The Long Struggle to Discovering Me

C000045602

Clara Meierdierks

Nee Uwazie

Editing and Layout: Amina Chitembo.
Cover Designed: Ahsan Chuhadry, Graphics Designer
Cover Art: Dr Vivian Timothy, Art Unleashed

Publisher: Diverse Cultures Publishing, UK.
www.diverse-cultures.co.uk
publishing@diverse-cultures.co.uk
Paperback ISBN: 978-0-9957396-1-1

Dedication

To my late mum Mrs Elizabeth Adanma Nneoha Uwazie, my late Father Patrick Uzodinma Uwazie, and my late sister Stella Nwanyinma Uwazie (†1999). And the rest of the family

To my husband Hagen, baby Ezinne, and my parents-in-law Christa and Alfred Meierdierks. I am where I am today because of our perfect teamwork. I could not have asked for a better family.

And to everybody out there trying to make meaning out of life. In God we stand, with God all things are possible.

Table of Contents

True love

First visit to his parents in Bremen

Relocating to Bremen, 2014

Bremen, Germany. a home for me

I have reason to smile again - our court wedding, April 2014

When God is at work - our church wedding, August 2014

Me with my parents-in-law

The bouquet

The wonders of God - the wedding ceremony

My wedding, a day to remember

My poem to my husband

Our wedding cakes

Happiness unmeasured - our bundle of joy, 2016

Thank God

A perfect team

When our desire turns hard

When the journey becomes tough, people whisper behind

Lessons for my readers - if you are reading this

Networking is very important

Not my way

Preface

"I'm here to spread a message of hope. Follow your heart. Don't follow what you've been told you're supposed to do."

- J. Cole.

The long struggle to discovering me is a book that I have decided to share with the world as a way of leaving my legacy. My life has been spectacular. I have experience immense joy like the birth of our special daughter Shanaya. I have also experienced immense pain. However, all through it, God has been on my side. This book would not have been possible without God.

I love poetry; you will find that this book consists of short poems, occurrences, and short passages which have been merged in order to make it more exciting and easier to read.

It is my great belief that we all have a story to tell. Like many before us who have shared their lives, I am writing this book with the hope of teaching someone something. We all can change a lot through sharing our life stories with others.

In this book, efforts have been made to recount memories that can never be replaced. Nothing is as good as being able to reproduce one's experiences from childhood.

Difficult as it was then, during my time growing up, we were able to make it memorable simply by using what we had. However, today it has somehow become more complex to see and watch kids growing up and see how the government mingles into some issues of parenting, which has both good and bad sides as to the upbringing of a child. And one can also see how technology and computers are gradually replacing the natural child play that encourages tolerance, communication and love.

Today, where one is born plays a big role in influencing the general well-being of a child. Culture is seen as paramount and it influences most of our thinking and adjustments into a new environment. There is nothing like living your culture while at the same time embracing other cultures. The world today is so diversified, and we need to accommodate others while retaining our roots. When everyone does that, the world will be a better place for everyone to live.

The long struggle to discovering me book is split into four section. It mentions some of the cherished traditions of our culture which were practised in both earlier times and in the late 1970s.

Most of these cultures were so rich in entertainment, they would make one want to run home at every opportunity.

Then, the system of the traditional Chief functioned, and the laws were respected, and orders reigned. I am from a family with a royal background, from Chief Onyekwere Eze Nfula la 1 of Mbaise, Imo State, the eldest brother of my grandfather. They formed one unified family, closely knitted together. For example, the crowning of Eze, the traditional marriage, the Christmas ceremony, Corpus Christi, JI Mbaise and the burial of an elderly person - these and some others not mentioned here in this book all remind me of the importance of one's culture. Unfortunately, most of these traditions are silently dying, or are being modernised. There is thus the increasing need and longing to revive and retain such ancient and beautiful traditions, and not simply modernise so many of our cherished traditions.

We do not choose where we are born or to what family we come into. This book takes us through what it means to be born in Africa with little or no opportunity, and where there was no room to accommodate minorities. Africa today is no longer the land that attracted the colonial masters in the 1800s.

We now experience an Africa that is so confused, faced with challenges, struggles, segregation and corruption, and with little or no room for its wards. This has led to so much suffering, hunger and disease, all being plagued with bad leadership. Life has become so difficult for the average African, especially in Nigeria where I come from. It is now also easier for youths to take the dangerous journey to other parts of the world, despite all of the uncertainties and dangers of migrating to the unknown. It is so easy for one to lose oneself in the presence of many challenges, and an easy way to slip into depression (a silent killer).

We all have dreams and we journey most times through rain and sun, taking various paths that are rough, with ups and downs, to get to realising our dreams. When we are faced with challenging situations, we either drown or swim out of them, as happened in my case. God is the reason why I made it this far and I am ever grateful and thankful to my family, Bola, Vivian, Sr. Gloria, Bunmi, Adanne and many others, as well as to those who gave me my negative experiences.

"For everyone we meet, experiences we encounter in life all have a role to play in making us or destroying us. In all, all depends on how we go about them".

- Clara Meierdierks.

PART I

MY ROOTS, MY CHAOS
MY CHALLENGES AND THE LOSS OF ME

"We have always held to the hope,
the belief, the conviction that there is a
better life, a better world, beyond the horizon"
- Franklin D. Roosevelt.

See my origins. I was born and brought up in Nigeria by the late Mr. and Mrs. Patrick Uzodinma Uwazie in Uwazie's compound. I come from a large family. There were five brothers, Chief Onyekwere, Uwazie, Agulanna, Eneremadu and Chima. As we were told, then they loved each other, they were so united and were each other's keeper - which is no longer the case today. I therefore have a royal background.

However, my country Nigeria is a land blessed with many natural resources, more than enough for even the future unborn generations. Nigeria is seen as the giant of Africa, with 36 states and a population of 195,461,430, which is equivalent to 2.5% of the total world population according to a UN estimate in May 2018.

It is the most populous country within OPEC, being located on the Gulf of Guinea in Africa. Since

1991, Abuja has been the capital of Nigeria. Nigeria has six geopolitical zones: the South East (consisting of the five states of Enugu, Imo, Ebonyi, Abia and Anambra), the South South (consisting of six states - Bayelsa, Akwa Ibom, Edo, Rivers, Cross River and Delta), the South West (consisting of six states - Oyo, Ekiti, Osun, Ondo, Lagos and Ogun), the North Central (consisting of seven states - Niger, Kogi, Benue, Plateau, Nasarawa, Kwara and FCT).

The North East (consisting of six states - Bauchi, Borno, Taraba, Adamawa, Gombe and Yobe), and the North West (consisting of seven states - Zamfara, Sokoto, Kaduna, Kebbi, Katsina, Kano and Jigawa).

Nigeria is said to be one of the many countries in Africa with plenty of natural resources, particularly precious metals, oil, natural gas, iron ore, lead, gold, coal, rock salt and others. There are also sufficient water and agricultural resources. However, for no reason that is plainly obvious, Nigeria has made itself dependent solely upon oil, since its first discovery in Olobiri, Bayelsa State in 1956.

MY LAND, MY HOPE.

I look forward into a great land,
A land that will respect and recognise all,

With no limitations, no discriminations,
On grounds of religion, language, tribe, sex or class.
But this is not the country I am seeing today.
All there is to see is a land where nothing is seen to
smile,
Where sighs, groans and unhappiness abound,
Roam and circulate in the air,
Where violence, anger and the killing of innocents
are the order of the day.
That land I loved so much,
Where is my land, my hope?

The great Nelson Mandela once said that the true terror is to wake up one morning and discover that your high school class is running the country.

Nigerians everywhere are very talented, but unfortunately the government either pretends not to know this or actually does not know this. I love Nigeria, but unfortunately Nigeria is a very corrupt country - rich, but with the highest number of poor people.

The country was under British rule for many years until her independence in 1960. Although colonisation did not overall do her well, to many eyes her independence is seen to be premature. Today nepotism, bribery and corruption has eaten deeply into Nigeria, a land of peace, hope and love. Many are forced to leave in search of greener pastures elsewhere. Its legislature, the civil service, the army, the police, the judiciary and the trade unions are not functioning effectively, and some would say they are not functioning at all.

There is total neglect for the masses, with high unemployment abounding. Consequently, many youths are leaving and sometimes taking extreme risks to try to come to Europe. Crime waves abound, with kidnapping at a high rate, so therefore its people live in fear as they feel ignored and neglected by the government that is supposed to protect them.

Nigeria is seen today as a beautiful blessed country plagued with coups, power tussles and economic woes. We need our green-white-green flagged country. I love my land, so God please help us to save it.

I was born in the Igbo tribe, we should love our countrymen. We should put hatred and selfishness aside and be our brothers' keepers.

I come from a side that is predominantly Christian - Igboland, a very friendly and tolerant tribe which is also very enterprising. It is located in the Southeast region, within the heart of business and the heart of a hardworking population.

The Igbo language is spoken by the Igbo people, being one of the three major languages spoken in Nigeria. The area of Igboland is reported to be densely populated, being estimated by the CIA World Factbook to have a population of about 32 million, and thus containing just less than 20% of all Nigeria's population (the South Eastern side from the River Niger is natively called Ndi Igbo).

Igbos are everywhere. They have been traced back to the time of the slave trade, as reported in history. The Igbos were skilled at trading, particularly with regard to the products from skilled craftsmen, as well as from local agriculture and the sales of yams, cassava, fruit, groundnuts and palm oil. Life was so good then, when no-one envied another, and peace and love reigned. Today;

"The centre can no longer hold again"
- Chinua Achebe.

AHIARA - MBAISE IN IMO-STATE

Ahiara is a city in Mbaise, situated about 16 miles between Owerri and Umuahia. It was the location of Chukwuemeka Odumegwu Ojukwu's declaration during the Nigerian civil war. A known catholic location, Ahiara is said to have been founded by a man called Odoji Amumu. 'Ahiara' is a type of plant, whose leaf means peace (Wikipedia). Some 89% of the population are catholic.

My home state, Imo state, is said (according to history) to have been named after the River Imo (Imo mmiri), with Otamiri and Njaba as tributaries. It was believed in olden times that the rivers were owned by deities and served as a means for fishing, transport and agriculture. I was lucky that my mama was well-informed and narrated stories to us when we were home. May and July are seen as very important months within Imo state, with the Festivals of the Goddess being celebrated, as the River Imo is said to often overflow its banks at these times. However, I have only read about this, not witnessed it happen.

We were told that the native people then believed very much in Mother Nature, before the initial coming of Christianity, and it worked well for them. There were beliefs about the Goddess of Fertility which were respected in Ngwa, Mbaise community, my province. The Imo river is said to be connected to Rivers state, Akwa Ibom, the largest river in Igboland (Okigwe) and to empty into the Atlantic Ocean.

The traditional beliefs and local system encouraged social justice and equality, with no discrimination and no segregation allowed. Igbo culture was very rich and involved many customs and practices, some were old and traditional, while others involved visual art and the use of language, and these all added to the beauty of my 'Igbo Land'.

The Igbo people, Nwere Madu, live in a land full of beautiful cultures and traditions, like the Yam Festival held annually on 15 August. I am so happy that the Mbaise people in Bremen celebrates JI Mbaise in Bremen every year with traditional dance, talks on the importance of preserving our heritage, culture, as well as being good Ambassador to the country where we live. I have great respect to Mr Madu Ukachi and Mr Chibuike Nwachukwu who have contributed immensely to the growth and survival of this great Mbaise union in Bremen. I have learnt much from them. Locally, the yam is a very important crop and it is usually the first to be harvested. Wherever one is, this is celebrated everywhere Igbos are found.

The Masquerade (Mmanwu, a kind of entertainment seen in celebrations), is said to still be respected. This was a happy event, where we awaited each time with high expectations. Everyone wanted to be at home, where joy, merriment and celebrations took place. The mask is said to resemble the spirit of the dead, and there were strongly-held beliefs that the spirits of dead loved ones watched over us. That is what the elders taught us in history, I witnessed it too.

The marriage custom (Iru mpede) is another great ceremony, where the bride-to-be is treated for three months in isolation. She is given all the care and attention she requires and generally well looked after, before she is officially handed over to the groom. The day of the marriage is always highlighted and graced with traditional rites, and crowned with peace, love and understanding,

The naming ceremony, when a new baby is born to any member of the family at home or abroad, is where all the local women gather in the person's compound and dance (Iti oro), this being a way of announcing the arrival of the new child. It is said to provide power which symbolises good wishes which are shared, being occasioned with dancing and merriment. These and lots of other beautiful traditions are gradually being neglected. We seem to be losing our roots and also losing our language.

MY LOVE FOR MY COUNTRY

Despite all that it has been through, Nigeria has produced a lot of stars, actors, artists and educated people, spread far and wide throughout the world. Indeed, Nigeria can be made great again, but first religion and politics need to be separated, to allow respect, dignity and equality for all Nigerians, without regard for sex, religion, tribe, language and class. Then one can begin to deal with corruption...

Nigeria has a lot of stars like King Sunny Ade, Sara Forbes Bonetta (the Yoruba slave who became Queen Victoria's daughter-in-law in 1843), and many others, including Sonny Okosun ('Which Way Nigeria' in 1984), Ik Dairo, Onyeka Onwenu ('Ekwe', 1984), Femi Anikulapo Kuti ('Zombie', 1977), Bobby Benson ('Taxi Driver'), to mention but a few.

Nigeria is also known for its artwork: stone carvings, wood, pottery and glass work. Bronze work can be seen in Enugu, considered by many as being the highest quality of ancient work, with Osogbo, Benin, Oyo Akwa Ibom all seen as the heart of wood carving, with Okigwe renowned for its pottery, along with Imo and Suleja, more information can be gotten from WIKIPEDIA. Our History should not be allowed to die down.

Cloth weaving and textile making is still loved and the Yoruba still use shrubs to create Indigo-coloured Batik-dyed cloth which is quite sensational. In the South, many women are employed in cloth weaving or textile making, while in the North, textile work is mostly dominated by men, either due to religion or local culture. However, the central areas of Abia, Oyo, Osogbo, Ife and Okene in Kogi state are still the most attractive centres for textile production. Who said Nigeria is not blessed?

THE NIGERIAN BRAIN DRAIN

Nigeria was once a country that could boast about having everything. But today Nigeria is so empty, so drained, where the future of many Nigerian youths is stagnant and threatened. Regrettably, Nigerian youths are leaving on a daily basis, although many are reported to have died, been imprisoned, sold as slaves in Libya, or even used for organ trading - what a terrible shame. God recognises good leadership and supports it. Whoever is designated as being the leader owes it to all to be a good leader. Unfortunately, Nigeria has not been all that lucky.

Nigeria in 2018 is facing its hardest time ever. We are in a democracy, but we pray for God to help us. People are killed every day, there is widespread hunger and poverty, and the gap between poor and rich people is widening every second. 'Which way my Nigeria', like Sonny Okosun sang in 1984.

Which way Nigeria?

Like Sonny Okosun, we love our fatherland and long to go back to that green-white-green flagged country. A land of love, peace and unity. Will there ever be that again?

LESSONS TO MY READERS

Wherever we are born, our roots cannot be replaced. We are who we are because of where we come from.

Home is home, and nothing will be like the original home where one is born.

Let us join hands to make our roots home and be good Ambassadors.

PART 2

MY CHILDHOOD

"Where my story takes me, however dark and difficult the theme, there is always some hope and redemption, not because readers like happy endings, but because I am an optimist at heart. I know the sun will rise in the morning, that there is a light at the end of every tunnel"

- Michael Morpurgo.

The happiest time,
funny and sincere,
In every childhood,
Where all were not written down,
but are stored somewhere,
away in memory,
unconscious,
ready for retrieval.
For report and storytelling,
Good and bad, fades
but not far away.
We remember something,
Always,
Things that shaped us,
Memories that broke us,
And people who held us together
And kept us going.

When emotions stir up,
When we feel lost,
And have no trace,
Our unconscious mind,
Our memory and storage
retrieves,
It is always there,
All we need do,
Is just a flashback,
And guess!
ready to be taken back,

Things we thought forgotten,
Things we think we're gone,
Ha! Never go missing,
Are always there,
To accompany us,
And serve as guide and measure,

We all have it, old memories,
Waiting for recall,
Use as a guide,
Good or bad memory
no matter, use well,
To make you a better person.

We did not have toys to play with, but we were happy,
Where we were, what we had was for us beautiful,

We had limitations set,
Rules were made,
Respect and humility reigned,
Love was our tie,
And together, we managed our ups and downs.

And all these embraced my childhood.

I am an original Nnarambia Ahiara Mbaise woman, a place where I grew up and which I love so much. I inherited a lot from my mum. We were continually under parental supervision, as our senior ones were trained early to assume motherly roles when our mothers were not there.

MY FAMILY
No matter what happens, family is the most important thing to be remembered. They may be difficult, wide apart, but they still find the common base.

John Wooden said that the most important thing in the world is family and love.

An umbrella that keeps us from getting wet
When it rains,
A tree with many branches spreads out for us,
A place where love never lacks.

We may all dance a different dance,
Family always make us feel wanted,

When we are lost,
Felt alone,
In trouble of any kind,
We all feel the branches,
Enveloping and shielding us,
That is family, for you and for me.
That is my family.

We had this family life, where aunts, grandparents and other relatives lived together and were bringing the children up together. It worked then, because there was no segregation, no hatred and no self-ishness. Everything went perfectly then, because children were considered everyone's responsibility to train.

My childhood experiences were very nice and have influenced me to this day in a very posi-tive way. I was born in a small village in Nigeria, Umuofor Nnarambia Ahiara in Ahiazu Mbaise, Imo state. I am proud to be an 'Mba-Five' woman, as popularly known. I don't care what stigma is attached by some regarding 'Mba-Five' people. Mbaise must be great again.

Unfortunately, some people don't really like us, as they say that Mbaise people are clever, hardwork-ing and are always alert. You see, these are qualities that are not always easily welcomed everywhere.

They will stigmatise Mbaise people until they also start seeing one another in a negative way, and it is sad to say that this is actually the case today. Ahiara is also associated with the 'Ahiara declaration', which made Ahiara very popular, until today.

I had a wonderful childhood. It was a nice time. There was not much bad to talk about in terms of my childhood, except the poverty. Well, we did not really see material and financial poverty then as a problem, because we felt so loved and protected by the family, and that is how it should be.

We only saw a close-knit family,
Full of love and ready to help one another,
We saw a mother, who gave all in love,
We saw a perfect world,
unpolluted despite all,
I longed for these times,
Today the world is so different.

WE MASTERED CHALLENGES EARLY

We could always do something with our friends after school. We learned to take responsibilities so early, as functions were divided amongst us and everyone knew what was expected of them. My family was loving, and we always kept together. Our mother was loving and caring, and that was what shaped me and my siblings very strongly, until today.

My mum was and still is my role model, even after her death on 1 April 2016. My mother was a teacher and she took me to school early as school was considered very important. In those early days of Nigeria, there was no social system, no direct help from the government to the family, so every family aspired for a good education for their children, as that was (and still is) the only strong weapon we could use to survive in Nigeria. Children are valued and are trained properly, so that they in turn take care of their older relatives.

My mama showed me early on how important school and education is and was. Faith had always played a significant and important role in the education of our mother. We grew up within the Catholic faith and are still volunteering today for the Catholic Church. Mama encouraged us to be obedient, to attend Bible classes, and be well dressed and decent when attending church. There was also quite a lot she would not tolerate from any of us at that time; for example, bad behaviour or dressing in a wayward manner.

We did not have much, but we were so happy. Farming then was seen to be practised by every family, so we helped and had enough to eat from our farm products. There was harmony within and between the families, and we could easily eat with another family with no fear. Life was indeed so blissful, worth living together. No wonder we progressed as we worked together for the good of all.

We had time to play with our mates, which was great, then when we came back from school we helped with the cooking, especially the girls. I was assigned plate washing-up duty, while my other sisters did the cooking and washing of dresses.

After eating we did our homework, tidied up, rested and, when evening came, we were so happy because when we were finished with the evening chores and had prayed within the family, we were allowed at least two hours to play in the compound. In those days, everywhere was safe. People trusted one another, and people had the fear of God in them. There were no quarrels and jealousy did not arise, as we were all our keepers. When there were disputes or quarrels, it was settled amicably and peacefully.

There was a local system which functioned then, which was based upon our respect for elders, transparency and not trying to manipulate the truth, as is the order of today. Today, centres can no longer hold together and there is anarchy, as described in Chinua Achebe's book, "*Things Fall Apart*" and "mere anarchy is loosed upon the world" (W.B. Yeats). Yes, things really have fallen apart, pretty badly.

OUR KIND OF EVENINGS

AND OUR PLAYING TOGETHER
We played with sand,
Had identifiable play, danced together,
Played together when it rained,
Jumped the rope,
Played Uka [Native play with clapping hands],
Hide and seek,
Danced, sang, just name it,

These were the most natural things. We were so happy, and the world was at peace. There was no crime, no fear of any kind, no competition and no superiority displayed. Perhaps there was, but we did not notice it. This was in the 1970s and 80s. How I wish for this time to return for our children. I am unsure whether our children, let alone our children's children, will ever experience the kind of freedom and love we had then. That was the time before the technology boom.

Today, playing on the computer, using Whatsapp and other social media has taken away our so natural social contact. People prefer to send text messages instead of having one-to-one meetings and telephone calls are almost gone, because one can easily WhatsApp - and that is it.

LOOKING BACK

Once in a while,
I looked up to this generation,
Emotions stirred,
Lost days come up,
Will they experience our joy?
Our kind of freelance and innocent days,
Our days of no technology,
When we had real love for one another,
When we cried and protected one another,
No competitions,
Leaders led well,
Children went to school,
There was free education,
Farms were fertile,
People loved their homes,
And no-one was in a forced exile,
No-one died on the road to Libya,
No story of Lampedusa,
And no mass graves of our youths.

When we were away,
We were happy to rush home,
To celebrate our Ji Mbaise,
Our Christmas was always a never-ending joy,
Not only because it was Christmas,

Because all family members were home,
The love and the joy.

Today, we will never experience such again,
because we have corrupt leaders,
No jobs for the youths and no hope.

How are we going to tell the younger ones?
That this type of time has gone,
What will they think of us?
That we offered them
Exile for the youths,
and death of our youths,
In search of a better tomorrow,
No good news for the unborn generation.
Unless we believe 'God will change the situation'.

I inherited a lot from my mom. We were continually under parental supervision, and the older ones were trained early to assume motherly roles when our mother was not there.

BIG SISTERS

For there is no friend like a sister in a calm or stormy weather, to cheer one on the tedious way, to fetch one if one goes astray, to lift one if one totters down, to strengthen whilst one stands.

My big sisters Franchesca and Angela took on the role of mother when mom was not there or was tired. The 'Adanne' as she is called, the first daughter in every family, is always so respected, as they are seen as a 'role model'. My Adanne Franchesca is one such person. She managed us well even in her young age. She assisted my mom, had a teacher training education and gained an appointment as a teacher. My sister Angela too. We were grateful as she played her part well, until she left for England in the 1980s.

When she left,
We felt the gap,
For her presence was unfilled,
Why?
In my eye, she is a perfect sister,
Generous with good heart.

She set us in hope,
And gave us good advice,
She supported mama,
Her kindness dominated,
Her soft way distinguishes,
The subtle.
Everyone respected and loved her,
For she was unique.
when she spoke her voice was welcomed.

MY MOTHER

Picture of my mum

*"I am closest to my mother, as she is my rock,
my pillar of strength, and my world.
Not only has she stood by me through all
times - happy, sad, and otherwise - but
there have even been moments when
I had completely lost hope, and her
immense belief in me had lifted me up"*

- Amruta Khanvilkar.

My mama was born Elizabeth Adanma Nwachukwu on 25 December 1926 into the family of Mr and Mrs Daniel Nwachukwu of Eziala Umuhu Okwuato in Aboh Mbaise, Local Government Area of Imo State. She was the first child and daughter of her parents.

She attended Gregory's Primary School, Umuhu Okwuato, where she obtained her first school leaving certificate in 1938. In those days, women were refused a Western education. Mama was humble, intelligent and God fearing. Her parents allowed her an education amidst the protest from their kinsmen. She then proceeded to a teacher training school, located at that time at Ogbor Nguru Mbaise from 1940-1942 and gained her first teaching appointment in 1942 at St. Theresa's Catholic School in Zaria in Northern Nigeria. Unforeseen circumstances brought her back to the Eastern region, but due to the unrest in the North she left for the East in 1963 and was reinstated as a Senior Teacher at St. Bridgid's Primary School with the help of Rev. Carter (the then Parish Priest) and through the help of my uncle Rev. Monsignor Vincent Uwazie, who was then a seminarian at the St. Peter and Paul Major Seminary, Ibadan.

Mama retired in 1984 and was among the lucky ones that received their Udoji salary arrears when Governor Mbakwe reigned (a Governor with good heart for his people). Mama was a devout Catholic, one who lived up to her devotion as a Catholic. She had challenges in her marriage, as my father had a second wife, and for several reasons' things weren't that smooth, but we give God all the glory.

Mama was a member of St. Brigid's Church Choir, the President of CWO of St. Theresa's group 9, the Nneyemaka (to help the poor), The Christian Sisters, St. Vincent the poor and other groups.

Mama got married to papa, the late Engr. Patrick Uzodinma on the 22nd of August 1949 in Kano. Their marriage produced eight children, two boys and six girls with two born quite late (Patricia and Stella Uwazie). Mama single-handedly brought us up. She was everything to us. She was a disciplinarian, peaceful, humble, religious and quiet to a fault. She represented Onu Obiri Nwugo well until her death.

Only a woman with the nerve of reinforced steel can go through what mama went through after her husband's death in the Nigerian civil war in 1967-1970.

Five years before her death in 2016, we all were home to celebrate mama's 85th birthday in December 2012, and then five years later mama died on Good Friday 1 April 2016 - she was born on a Friday, went into a coma on a Friday, died on a Friday and was buried on a Friday.

The death of her three loving junior brothers broke her heart (De Bernard, De Nich and De Francis Nwachukwu); may their souls continue to rest in peace. Amen.

As if she knew she was dying, the day before she fell into a coma, I spoke with her on the telephone to reassure her that another grandchild for her was on the way. Her answer was "Nne gi akawalanka" "Your mom is getting old" and she told me as if she was begging, "Umum unu ekwe kwa la ka Ihere mem Maam Nwuoo, li ma kwa num" ("My children, you people should not allow me to be buried shamefully"). This is so because the tradition or rather the people have turned burial into a kind of competition, which it should not be at all.

Thank God, we gave her a befitting burial, and everything went peacefully and everyone praised us, as we give all the glory to God. My greatest joy was that she blessed me and my husband during our visit home in 2015.

MAMA'S PICTURE

Sweet mother,
Sweet memory,
Weary then,
Thorned with misfortune,
Weighed with burdens.

Spirit shined,
Embraced and mastered
Her challenges
She did not bury those thoughts,
With them she fought on.

What happened, happened,
Loss of my father,
Death of her hero,
As she was left with eight children,
To care and train,
O! mother full of care,
I did not understand more then,
In my mind dear mother
My nature's copy,
My comfort.

How I wish I could bring you back
To give you the homage you deserved,
And make strong and good the ills,
Of my childhood.

I could give all to bid you back,
But you are in good hands
With the Lord,
your exit on the first of April 2016.

This day,
They called me that the light
Struck away,
That your spirit fled.

My best half is gone to the Lord,
And I mourned and cried like a child,
And refused to be consoled.
My thought crippled,
Bounded, confined and paralysed,
Doubts and fears overtook me.

Thanks mama,
For your kindness,
Your sacrifice,
The lessons you taught us,
I mingled easily with the world,

Because you taught me some values,
Which I will give over.

My mother was and is the best, most loving and most devoted mother. In her time, she raised us all with love and conviction. My mother was the most important person in my life. A quiet mother, helpful to us and other people. She was honest and taught us the most important things in life. Love you ever mama.

MY FATHER

> *"I cannot think of any need in childhood as strong as the need for a father's protection"* (Sigmund Freud).

Unfortunately, I did not get to know my father because he fell in the Nigerian civil war, towards the end of the war as I was told, around 1969/70. My siblings have told me a lot about him - that he was a helpful and caring man who had helped so many people within and outside the family in his time.

TO MY DECEASED FATHER

Picture from papa
Though you were gone,
months before I was born,
Though I did not get to see, experience and feel you,
I got something from your genes,
Something which I am told about you,

Something that made me long for you,
I did not see your face,
But I have your picture,
Hath nature not taken you early, we would
Have been a good team,
You would have walked the road with me,
And showed me your own values,
You would have given me another
type of home,
Joined mama to make a home for all of us,

I would not lie,
There were moments I wished you were there,
To take my hands, play with us,
But death snapped you early,

You fell in the Biafran war,
A hero that was never recognised,
In a nation where lives were less valued,

I value you as I pay you homage,
My hero, whose half gene I carry along.
You were supposed to be my first hero,
You were supposed to be available,
To believe in me,

You went,
Away, far away,

Not your fault,
I love you Papa.

Papa continue to rest in peace.

We read about the Biafrans as being courageous,
their deaths as a big loss. What was told and what
was written in history stand to remind us all that
war is never a solution to anything. It brings about
endless loss of life, pain and unending agony. The
Biafran war then was not seen as a movement of
Ibo, Ibibio, Ijaw or Ogoja, described as nationalism
seeking for equality. Whatever let there be peace.

POVERTY

> *"Survival was my only hope,*
> *success my only revenge"*
>
> *- Abraham Lincoln.*

Poverty, a no name for the rich,
Unexpected in life,
Though a loyal companion for the poor,
That hinder cheers and celebrations,
Bared us, chained and enveloped.

Who can be questioned for your unkindness,
A mischance you are

Lay blame on anyone,
But don't grace me anymore.

I pray you,
Keep far away from me,
Touch not my effort,
Or else you shall offend my progress,
I will offend you
With passion
And regard you less,
With all boldness, hard work and prayers.

You might appeal to others,
Dare look not on me again,
I experienced you,
I know your hold,
You paint fear with your hidden daggers,
Which corruption gave you
To hinder good works, terrorise youths,
And kill good efforts.

Authorised by my prayers,
I shall shame you, trash you,
And send you to the abyss,
Where you will neither touch nor destroy,
My fellow people I bid all to follow suit,
And thrash all paths to poverty.

God help us!

My most horrible experience was poverty in Nigeria. My mother and my older sisters had to work so hard to enable us to get education and training. My mother often refrained from eating so that we could eat something. I secretly cried a lot and vowed hard to learn and work to show my mother how grateful I am and to be able to fulfil a better and easier life.

I'm quiet, handle stuff calmly. I am combative and never give up easily. For what I am and what I can do I am so infinitely grateful to God and my mother.

As children, we learned so much from my mother, to be good and obedient, to be punished if we behaved badly, and our mother explained why. The fear of poverty has always accompanied us, the uncertainty of where the next food would come from. The openness in the family was part of our education and has welded us together in poverty and in all other things - we are very much together in what still exists today and is lived. We have learned that family is the highest good. That's why, despite poverty, I grew up caring and sharing. Family and trust is for me a building block to caring. Mama has given us her precious and dear love. I wish this feeling to all people in the world. Because love means trust, understanding, hope and much more. I felt very loving.

There was never a dispute with our parents. Because mama had sacrificed so much for us, we learned to treat her with care and respect. There was simply no competition within the family. We always kept together and for each other, which is still the case today. Even outside the family, at school and in professional life, there was never any so-called competition. We have learned to be ambitious and purposeful.

Sexual or Social Enlightenment and Culture
"A very important lesson but was never considered important for us."

Sexual enlightenment was not a big issue, since the mentality and culture in my country Nigeria, as well as a Catholic education, does not permit such. As long as one is unmarried then this was not allowed, nor any kind of contact, what our culture called "careless social contact".

Unwanted pregnancy and abortion were frowned upon - parents were excommunicated from the church and treated everywhere with scorn. Such people were considered to be 'the black sheep of the family'. Any sex at all was seen as taboo. We were not even told about or prepared towards our menstruation. I remember vividly that when I had my first menstruation, at twelve years of age, I was in school and I remember that I went to the toilet during playtime at my school, the Central School Nnarambia Ahiara. It was pit toilet in those days, and suddenly I discovered I was bleeding. I became so scared and could not tell anyone, for the fears of misinterpretation. I used toilet paper, but before I got home I was stained with blood.

Little did we knew then what menstruation was all about, that it was the monthly period in every woman before the menopause. Perhaps our culture prevented my mom from letting me know more about sex as an important lesson, but that was not good for most of us.

It was when she saw me with blood stained cloth that my mom took me into the house, helped me to clean myself and sat me down. That was the first time I was hearing about this monthly bleeding. She said to me that, from today, should any man sleep with me, that I would become pregnant and consequently that I should avoid bringing any disgrace to the family. This made me distance myself from my male counterparts, because we kind of believed that one could become pregnant even through merely being looked at or by simply being touched.

Well, I did not miss anything, because you don't miss what you do not know. Life was, in my eyes, very beautiful. However, from today's perspective, I would act out this situation quite differently, preferring an orderly education.

There has never been a desire for separation, since we have learned to respect each and every one of the family through our education and faith as an independent personality.

The family relationships and the importance of school and professional life was so important to my mom. How important this would be, as we understood quickly and absorbed everything offered us through both our formal and informal education. How important the family is was also shown to us, because we supported each other mutually, since mama took me to school early and showed me the way to schooling and learning.

My relationship with my mother was very loving and never changed until her death in 2016, nor has it changed since. Even when I left Nigeria to study in Germany, the bond had actually intensified even though the distance has become bigger. Both my sister who lives in London and I have continued to show the respect and the love that mama gave us way back then. All the expectations mama put into us children have come true, because she wanted us all to have a loving and better life.

MY CONFUSION

> *"Feelings are something you have,*
> *not something you are"*
> *- Shannon L. Adlder.*

I did not understand many of my mother's decisions back then, because at the time I was a teenager. I wanted to do things differently than my mom did. She always explained her decisions to me and tried to make it clear to me, no matter what my own decisions were, which I then had to master with full force. We never had to justify our decisions because, as a family, we respected and supported everyone in all things, even if a path was not that easy.

A good and virtuous lesson from my mom,
In an age of rebel,
When thoughts were in confusion,
And tendencies were there,
Advice was half accepted,
And protest,
Hands would be all to guide
An age of rebel.

It is this, I mean
That age of vulnerability,

That oppose wills,
That are obeyed.

In nature,
Fall of many youths,
That allowed that vulture in them
Devour, and win,
Into power that rebels old and young,
And betray future.

Today I have a flashback,
In the way I reacted sometimes,
I acted in many ways that empowered me,
Truth from my soul,
God above
For now,
My soul reconciles.

NOTE: There were things I would want to do differently today. Cherish your family, enjoy your parents and be useful to yourself, because in the end, without them we would not have seen the light of day. Let's be good to our parents, no matter who they are.

PART 3

MY PEERS AND OUR SCHOOL DAYS

Those people who help form us

"It's rather like attending a university seminar where you are talking to a few gifted specialists who deliver a paper to an audience of their peers. That's one way of making music" (Garvin Bryans).

O proper group,
That shape and mar,
Good for growing
I never lacked,
boast the pleasure,
sent orders going,
forced trees to speak,
So strong are peers.

I had a happy experience as a child and I enjoyed the company of those I then called my peer friends. We were six good friends within the family - Patricia, Emilia, Cecilia, Ngozi, Ego, but the closest to me was Nwada. Although she was older than me, our friendship was like her protecting me. Emilia was also very good to me, and Ego was also very understanding.

We identified with each other, everyone played a role in my life. Nwada da Wancha (as I call her) was like a tree to me, as she protected me and defended me against all things. Her family became my second home. Whenever I went to their house, even when she was not around, her mum made sure I had something to eat, the same way as when she came to visit our house.

We identified with our social habits and manner of dressing. This was a beautiful stage for us, with a lot of abundant memories, of truly old and young.

The 1970s, those were very beautiful years for us. We made a special impact without knowing, being choir members, Legion of Mary in the church. We also took an active part in the community, cleaning the roads, the church and helping in every way, even with the farm work.

I could go on and on recalling. There was this functioning chieftaincy itself, with rules that were obeyed. We cherished it all, and we could re-explore it over and over again. But more important were our people and their kind of discipline, the characters then were very pure and respectful with love.

Nwada was like my right-hand sister and she played a very crucial role in my life. There was this big sister role, while between us was a gap in our age, which was not a problem for our sisterly friendship. These memories cannot be replaced, these essential situations. This is not to say that there were not others then in my life, but in her case, her late mom da Wancha would always make sure I was well cared for whenever I came over to them. My mom liked Nwada so much - we were just like from the same parents.

Of course, there were times we were tempted to party with others secretly. Once we tried to sneak through the fence, but we were caught, taken home and flogged, and never did we try it again.

"The best and most beautiful things in the world cannot be seen or even touched - they must be felt with the heart"

(Helen Keller).

As a child we all depend on our parents to encourage us to have an interest in school. I remember when my mom used to take me to her class, and I was treated like madam's daughter in school. However, my mom did not allow us have any special preferences because of her. We were just like other kids and that was good for us at this early stage.

We were given assignments and were supported to learn how to solve problems and find solutions. At the end of school, we were given homework to take home. The next school day this homework was checked and corrected.

There was no pressure to rush through anything, so therefore we understood the lessons that we were taught. Our questions were attended to, the children were watched and monitored, and when we did something wrong, we were punished, but importantly the reasons were explained to us.

Children were for everyone, as we were meant to understand, and it was a general duty to train a child, even those who were not your own. As long as it was done in good faith, parents were not angry.

Some days were longer than others in school. Parents were happy to see their children in school uniforms, neatly dressed. Mischiefs were watched, curtailed and reported. At the end of school, we were all happy to rush home, because we knew it was full of love. And also, we could do a lot at home, and with our peer groups. Our time was really fun.

Education was at that time, until secondary school level, free. Skills like carpentry and furniture-making were taught. Farming was a family business then, so people had to work hard but had enough to eat. We were encouraged to spend our time wisely.

At the age of twelve I passed my common entrance examination to go to secondary school. In those days, there was far less corruption. People's hard work was recognised, with entry into secondary school being based on merit and no bribes were expected or given, unlike today. Gross enrolment rate never exceeded net enrolment.

Every child followed the school programme and was expected to conform like in the UK, because at that time Nigeria still followed the British system of education. This was adhered to and there was no room to join a secondary school at a later age. The repercussion of starting school late or not at all is still a great problem in Africa generally, and specifically in Nigeria, when in present times many students end up dropping out of school because they feel shy, insulted or bullied.

Those who fail to remain in school often end up going into crime if not properly guided, or enter the cheap labour world, where their productive lives in most cases are limited.

Today, there are so many international schools in urban centres and in the capital city Abuja, the commercial capital of Nigeria. Most are boarding schools. For those who can afford it, these schools follow the educational systems of Britain or America or follow the International Baccalaureate standards. They provide a good quality of education, being mainly well equipped. The school year in Nigeria runs from January to December, from 8.00am to 3.00pm. Fees, school uniform, books, extra activities, transport and other associated costs are all included in these private school fees.

Getting to these very good schools is highly competitive. Preference is given to some nationalities, tribes, organisations, government bodies and to the rich or influential families. This is sad, as there are no places for poor people, and this should not be.

I passed the Common Entrance examination and subsequent interviews before getting into secondary school. In 1978 I was admitted into Obohia Technical School, Ahiara, where I studied for two years before leaving for St. Louis Girls Grammar School, Ikere Ekiti, Ondo state, Nigeria.

LIVING HOME FOR THE FIRST TIME

Most decisions made for us, or made by us, lead us somewhere. My late mother had to struggle to pay for our secondary school fees. On one occasion, in 1981, my uncle who is now a Monsignor but was then a Rev. Father in one of the Catholic parishes in Ondo, came home one day and decided to take me to the St. Louis Girls Grammar School, Ondo state. The Rev. Sr. Patricia was then the school principal, and that made it easy for me. She was a kind-hearted ordained Catholic Reverend sister, very angelic and a general mother. She came from my village of Nnarambia Ahiara, Imo state.

I was happy at their decision, but at the same time I felt so lonely. I struggled with these feelings. Each time the thoughts came up, I tried to suppress my fears of leaving to go to another entirely different state, tribe and language. Although English is our common language in Nigeria, you are still expected to speak your own native local language, which in my case is Yoruba.

Knowing full well that it was not going to be easy adapting, I was determined to follow my uncle's advice.

As the fateful day of leaving approached, worries and sleepless nights plagued me. I was torn between whether I should say 'No'. I would be leaving my loving mom, my siblings, my peer friends and my holy family that was so dear to me. I cried and cried, but still held on to my uncle's plan to take me out of our land. What was most important to me was that I needed to make this journey, no matter how difficult it might be.

On that fateful day in 1981, on this fateful day, we left home. Both my family and I cried like I was going away forever. My uncle's driver drove us, and throughout the journey, I still contemplated going back home. I was so fearful, but I had to go through with it. I wish I could have made it easier then, but there was no way, no short cut.

The journey lasted a whole day, and we arrived at Ondo, my uncle's parish, late in the night. I was exhausted not only from the journey, but also from all my crying.

My uncle had some maids, and two of them came from our neighbouring village. That made it a bit easier for me on arrival. Their names were Ndidi and Immaculata.

It was on a Friday. The plan was for me to stay the weekend with my uncle and proceed afterwards to the convent to my new grammar school. You cannot Imagine my fear at the thought of going to meet totally strange people. First in the convent. Thoughts of how to compose myself, how to recite all the prayers.

On the Sunday my uncle De Vin, as we called him, with his driver took me to St. Louis Girls Grammar School, Ikere Ekiti, in then Ondo state, where we were received by a smiling Rev. sister with a beautiful dentition (gap teeth). The smile and her warm reception took some of my fears away from me. I was later to find out more about Da Patti, a very fantastic and kind-hearted human being. I had seen her before in our village, but that was some years back before this particular day.

I made friends easily, and tried to talk about home and my loneliness. However, I struggled with learning the Yoruba language. Then I met Bola who was very good hearted and kind. This changed my attitude and I was able to adjust.

I also struggled with a lot of other things. We stayed in the boarding school, where students were from near and far, mostly with students from families that had famous names. I was privileged through my uncle to be in this school. It was a highly disciplined school with a good name, and it was also highly competitive. We wore a white and light blue uniform which I was so proud of. We began every morning with daily mass before classes, while readings and singing in the church were rotated among us.

The Christmas period was a great occasion for us. I partook in most of the activities and inter-house sports. I was very good then at the high jump, throwing the javelin, and volley ball. In fact, it was such a great time spent. We had prep time, and things were all in order. With time I made other new friends. People used to call me 'Omo Sister Patti', that is Sister Patti's daughter. I enjoyed the kind treatment from some of my colleagues.

In 1983, our group sat the West African School Certificate Examination (WAEC). I gained 5 credits, but unfortunately only attained a p7 in English which was compulsory for every admission into a higher school. The same year I sat my GCE examination (General Certificate of Education) and fortunately completed my credits.

Most of my friends and colleagues gained admission to the university straight away, but I lost one-year waiting. I initially wanted to study law, but somehow along the way I had an encounter that changed my world. I became very passionate about being a nurse. I loved the uniform, white, with a cap. Eventually, in 1985, I got into my passion, via the School of Nursing, Ondo.

Training School

"A dream doesn't become reality through magic; it takes sweat, determination and hard work"

- Colin Powell.

On getting to Ondo, since there was no boarding system at the school, my uncle asked me to stay with the school matron who was from Cameroon and married to a Nigerian. I underwent hard training with her. I was more or less a house girl. We had a bore-hole in the compound, which was not connected upstairs and I had to go every time to fetch and fill containers upstairs with water used for cooking, washing and flushing the toilets. I did this for over two years. I also washed and ironed, went shopping, cooked and did all that a maid does.

I cried because that wasn't the kind of life I had envisioned for myself at this stage. I still had to make time to prepare for my school work. She did not allow me to bring my school friends home, and I felt even more isolated and very lonely.

In 1986, some information reached us that our school was going to be merged with the Akure School of Nursing, I was so delighted, so happy to leave that environment and to lead a normal school life. Of course, the matron did not like the idea, but for me it was such a huge relief.

I have this wonderful friend. Bunmi Korikor (now Falusi), who is very nice. We agreed to look for a room together. She accepted me, and we were like sisters. We would spend some weekends at her place in one of the villages in Ondo state. I got to know her family quite well and I felt more secure. We could also visit my uncle in Ondo.

In 1988, we finished our training at the School of Nursing and entered the labour market. I obtained work as a Registered Nurse at the Lagos Medical

Centre, Ikeja. I worked for several years there and then went for my midwifery training to Zonkwa Kaduna state in the Northern part of Nigeria. I was 25, a very ripe age, when I gained admission. I had migrated all through my life.

We had a routine, because it was attached to a convent and our principal was a Reverend Sister. I had to cope with a new environment, new people and a new language, which was Hausa. Because our training and practical work was going to involve the native people, we were bound to learn the basic language, learn to eat some of their local foods and so on.

I felt so estranged and sad again. So real and so close to the point of going back to Lagos where I had my friends. This was in 1991 and I had just started a one-year programme. There was no easy way of communicating with my home then, except by actually physically going back home. Somehow, I ran into an uncle, Mr. Eze from Amaokwe, a neighbouring village to ours. He is deceased now, may his soul rest in peace, Amen. He was so helpful to me, he gave me foodstuffs, and sent his children and wife to see me in school. They also taught me some key Hausa words, although I seem to have forgotten them all now.

There was no reason to feel alone again now. He was going home from time to time and I was so grateful that I was in touch with home.

I participated actively in school, both in seminars and in out-of-curriculum activities, I loved doing midwifery work, the joy of seeing healthy mothers and their babies. I was awarded the Best Student/Best Behaved Student Award and felt so proud and happy, and I was so grateful to my God.

I graduated in March 1991 and went back to stay at my cousin Caro's place in order to look for a job. During this same year I was employed at several clinics, but with 'peanut' pay; the Ikeja Medical Centre, the Dialysis Centre in Ikeja, and at the Ikoyi Medical Centre as a Nurse/Midwife. After four years doing such low-paid work, in 1995, I had to resign my current job to travel for the first time to Germany to take care of my Auntie Cyrene Eneremadu, who battled with cancer until her death in late 1997, all sponsored by Uncle Dr. Nich Uwazie in Grevenbroich, Germany.

MY JOURNEY TO GERMANY

"Every great dream begins with a dreamer. Always remember, you have within you the strength, the patience, and the passion to reach for the stars to change the world"

- Harriet Tubman.

I went through this with hope. Every decision we take in our lives, even the smallest thing, will have a good or bad effect. In one of my chapters in the AWE book, I elaborated upon 'my pains of migrating to Germany' - the rough times, my hopes, the dash and the fight to continue. I placed all my hope in God, and there were so many good people who accompanied me during this rough time.

No journey is easy, no new chapter is without fear, fight and perseverance, remain the backbones.
Forget the rollings, rise up,
Stay firm, hold on to God,

"Few things in the world are more powerful than a positive push. A smile. A world of optimism and hope. A 'you can do it' when things are tough"

- Richard M. Devos.

Endurance, Patience, and Struggle

"Life is a song - sing it. Life is a game - play it. Life is a challenge - meet it. Life is a dream - realize it. Life is a sacrifice - offer it. Life is love - enjoy it"

- Sai Baba.

In 1997 my aunt, Mrs. Cyrene Eneremadu (Nee Uwazie), was diagnosed with cancer. This was the very first time that the family had been struck down with such news. My uncle, Dr Nich Uwazie, arranged for her to be treated in Etienne Krankenhaus, Neuss. I had to resign my job as a nurse at the Ikoyi Medical Centre, Lagos, Nigeria and travel to Germany to take care of my sick aunt. It was not an easy journey.

While in Germany, my uncle's wife Irmtraut, a very good German woman, God sent, took care of us, drove us around, and organised my Auntie appointments because I did not understand the language. She did a lot with us, as my uncle was always on business trips then. After her treatment in Germany we came back to Nigeria, but sadly we lost my dear aunt six months after arriving home. She had metastasis and died in the Ogbor Hospital, in Imo State, may her soul continue to rest in peace, Amen.

Unfortunately, she never had a good life in marriage, because her husband treated her quite badly. Because of her trust in our culture, her home and religion, she endured, because we were taught to endure in marriage.

Her death from cancer was devastating news for all of us, because we were a close-knit family.

After her burial in her husband's compound in Mbutu Mbaise, everyone departed to their various places and that was when it dawned on me, I felt so empty, so alone, with no job and no plan, there was no money - what was I to do?

I did not know how to learn the acts of endurance, patience and total trust in God. In time I did, as I realised that prayers were going to be my source of consolation. I cannot count how many buckets of tears poured out of me during the subsequent weeks and months. Sometimes, I lay back and drifted off to sleep like a baby.

As I woke up, the thoughts came flooding back. I drank the tears of pain, I watched pain pierce my soul, and I failed to keep control. It lingered on, and I couldn't tell the difference between day and night. My life became uncertain and unbearable. I hated this feeling of helplessness, but what could I do?

"No dream is too big. No challenge is too great. Nothing we want for our future is beyond our reach"

- Donald Trump.

I couldn't give up. I had to carry on. I thought about our Lord Jesus on his journey to Calvary on

Good Friday; each time He failed, He got up and carried on. I asked Him for the inner strength to get up and move on and not sit in self-pity. I told myself that I must try harder and pray harder for the help that I needed. Thank God for the gift of good friends. Bola, my true friend, helped to ease the pains of my life journey, for which I am ever grateful to her.

Lost in Thoughton My Way Back to Germany

"Remember your dreams and fight for them. You must know what you want from life. There is just one thing that makes you dream become impossible: The fear of failure"

- Paulo Coelho.

In the quest to find my feet, I realised that I had a multiple-trip visa for Germany and, with my friend, we made plans for me to return to Germany. I had to look for people who would lend me money, because I did not have anything except for the 500 Deutschmarks which my uncle had given to me. I changed them, but it was not enough for my ticket.

I discussed the situation with my brother Cosmas, who spoke to a family friend. We both went to the Okoko side of Lagos, Nigeria, where Mr. Uzo lived. I remember vividly how he welcomed us. His wife and children were so lovely. I told him about my ordeal, and he and his wife immediately agreed to help me. Of course, I promised to repay them as soon as I got to Germany, because I went with the thought of just getting there and obtaining a job immediately; that was my mentality then. I did not realise what going back to Germany without money and knowledge of the language would mean for me. I felt so relieved that one part of the problem was solved. He gave me fifty thousand Naira, and as that was a time when our economy was still fair, with this I was able to buy my ticket.

I arrived in Germany with my heady dreams and hopes of working and helping my family. Little did I know of the many challenges that lay ahead.

First was the failed attempt to convert my tourist visa to a student visa. This was a very bitter experience for me and I had to leave Germany and fly back to Lagos. This broke my heart, for not only had I needed to borrow the first money for my trip, I was now having to go back to face the person who lent me the money.

It was in 1997 that all these things happened. However, with the help of my great friend Bola, who pressed all the right buttons for me, I finally, in April 1998, found my way back to Germany as a student.

I was so elated and thought I could adjust easily, but the fight and struggle continued throughout my first year at the University of Mannheim to study German and English. I battled with keeping up with the German courses, although I excelled in the English courses. At some stage I was torn between going back to practise as a nurse, but the problem then was that I did not have the necessary papers or work permit.

However, somehow, I was able to sort out how to do all of the coursework. I had to face many challenges along the way of course, but after about five years I finally got by permanent visa to remain in Germany and my work permit. God knows how excited and thankful I was.

A long rough journey, for those with God, patience and perseverance

"Life is a dream for the wise, a game for the fool, a comedy for the rich, a tragedy for the poor"

- Sholom Aleichem.

THE TWO THAT WERE INSEPARABLE

Chioma is my childhood friend and sister. We grew up together in Mbaise. Faith brought us together through my uncle, now Monsignor Uwazie, who was a friend of the family, and this friendship extended, and we became more like a family. Both families were alike. We witnessed our childhood challenges together.

At the time when I left for Ondo state, our communications were irregular, as at that time there were no possibilities of having regular telephone calls. We were apart, but not lost in thought. She also travelled to Germany while at quite a young age, so around that time we were all very busy.

In late 1998 and early 1999, I had terrible difficulty getting back into the system as a nurse. To follow my dream, the German language poised a huge challenge for me. It was at this point I opted to leave for the United States. I obtained admission to study for a B.Sc. nursing degree at California State University, paid the school fees with the help of my uncle, but was then refused a student visa.

In September 1999, I travelled to attend an interview at the US Embassy at Ikoyi, Lagos, Nigeria. While I was preparing for the interview, my brother Cos was with me at Auntie Theresa's place in Okoko, Lagos, where she was then living with her family.

Auntie Da Terry was my hero - an auntie with a good heart. Unfortunately, she did not receive very fair treatment in her husband's house. However, she endured and used her good character with prayers to endure all of the confrontations. Today she is a blessed mother with four lovely children, all settled in the USA, with her first daughter Chioma married with a son and holding a new Ph.D. qualification, what a grace.

While in Lagos we received the message that my sister Stella had just had a miscarriage but had complications. She was treated in the hospital, but when there was no improvement she demanded to be brought home. I remember speaking with her and reassuring her. "Da Stella", I said to her, "Hold on, I am in Lagos". I promised her we would be seeing her the next day, after my interview. Instead, my cousin Joachim came with the news that she had died during the night.

Here I am, no visa, my sister has just died, my immigration case is lingering. Can anyone imagine what questions I asked God!

I had no option. We left for the village the next day, arrived home and prepared for her burial. Afterwards I left for Germany to sort my papers out. While home I was able to get Chioma's number. I had, with the help of my friend Bola, made all the right moves to get my immigration sorted out.

Nothing ever came easy for me. Storm upon storm. I arrived in Germany with the idea of calling Chioma. She was so glad to hear my voice. I told her about my ordeals and she asked me to come down to meet her in Augsburg. We were so happy about this reunion.

We have had a long story together, a long way, we share a lot together, our ups and downs, our roots. We quickly decided upon what to do. Life was not easy for her either. She also had had several challenges with her immigration, but the good news was that we were both there and could support one another. She had her job at Alpenhof in Haunstetten, Augsburg, and I was on and off travelling to Mannheim, Grevenbroich, in the bid to sort out my papers.

Bola may God continue to bless you, a very dear friend.

I eventually had a base in Grevenbroich, but also had a second address in Augsburg with my sister Chioma Vivian. With her family at Fritz Wendel Straße in Augsburg, I found again my lost second home. Branko, her husband, a good-hearted man. This made life so much easier for me. The birth of her son Jason united us even more strongly than we were previously. I was like a second mother to Jason. Life was going fine for me, because I had a job at Wetterstein Altenheim in Augsburg - not what I had wanted, but I needed the job and the money it brought in.

It was with them that my writing became so intensive. They would tease me, which we laughed about.

I stayed and worked in Augsburg from 2000 through to 2004, until I was forcefully asked to go back to Grevenbroich because of my immigration status. I have previously elaborated upon this in the chapter I wrote in the AWE book (The pains of Migrating to Germany).

Today I say to God be the glory, because I know that God will never give us a cross that we can never carry.

IN DILEMMA AGAIN

"Let your hopes, not your hurts, shape your future"
- Robert H. Schuller.

All my life, I have known this lady in me that had rough ways of doing things. Even when in a relationship I was like someone who was destined to face thorns in everything I did. Falling in and out of relationships, my relationships were not holding. It was just like I was bewitched. But trying to find out why wasn't then my concern.

In reality, I was so angry, sad within myself at some of the decisions I had taken. Such decisions have come to shape my life. But unfortunately, I could not then understand such things.

I was kind of coming out of one problem and jumping into the next. Is this really human?

This shook my faith, made me question things a lot. I did not know what was actually going on in my life. I confided my thoughts with my family, my sister, Da Franca, Sr. Gloria, Vivian all who were closest here with me. I became depressed. I hated myself and was so ashamed of who I had become.

People did not spare me, they killed me with their gossip, I was dead and back. And the doubts continued within me.

Was I meant to go down this lane?
To fight this fight,
To tear these thorns or get thorned?

Some people have it rough. I happen to be one of those people.

2004 after my long struggle with my immigration papers here, when I thought It was over,
When I felt the sun was rising again,
Slam, another thing was waiting, a bigger bridge to cross.

I met this guy along my struggle,

A black guy, one would think...

'Everything seemed good, until they started pinching.

I thought it was a perfect relationship, I failed to see the bridge.

2008 to 2014 were very challenging years once again for me. Was it a chosen course of life? Now I respect people in a battered relationship. While there, as with my case then, I knew that a lot was wrong, but as a matter of principle and thought of the society I was in, I swallowed a lot. Today, I cannot explain why I stayed and tolerated so much.

From the time of my encountering this guy until the time we broke up, it could all be described as hell. It was so hard for me; every path I took towards knowing me became harder. 'Why?' kept on recurring, yet I could not give myself any answers.

> *"Learn from yesterday, live for today, hope for tomorrow. The important thing is not to stop questioning"*
>
> *- Albert Einstein.*

My full acceptance of this relationship was hampered by many people. There are some people, sisters and in-laws, who think they have the upper hand in African marriages. When you meet a 'I should be obeyed' type of in-law, you know you are in for a real battle and struggle to be accepted in a place you want to call home. I had this experience.

Oh, I had a dance with the devil, in a woman's form. She, today, I pray that God touches her heart so that she sees more the inside and not the outside of people, Oh! I tell you, she was a thorn bird, a real one!

During this time, what kept me sane was - academia.

I read a lot, enrolled myself in a lot of academic programmes, ran distance programmes with the university, and attended workshops and further training. I gained lots and lots of qualifications, and as you know 'pursuit of knowledge costs money'. The truth was I did not even feel it, and yet at the same time I was financially tasked to help start a business.

I was so hard working. Since I earned more than him, it was not a problem, I took care of most of the financial responsibilities, as it should be. There was no reason for 'mine' and 'yours '. He was so crude in his way of thinking and had this mentality that the woman should face only the problems arising in her husband's home and not her family. Imagine after going through all my ordeals to find myself in this mess!

Talking about helping my family was a taboo, because their culture said so, he would tell me. It was like I had a speck in my eyes. So many bad things happened, so many incidents were created out of nothing, and I was reduced, and yet I went through all these. A lot I can't even narrate here.

I did not understand me, did not know what I was looking for in that relationship, I had my German passport already, so what was I doing in a battered relationship? I did not know.

The worst part of this was that I thought the worst was over. No! This was worse than what I had previously thought of as being the worst. Then it got worse again.

I borrowed money in my name. First with Hypovereinsbank In Düsseldorf, which I handed over to him, then a second and third time from Postbank, we went together. Huge amounts of money, for which I was the sole signatory, these we agreed to use to start a construction business in Nigeria.

We went together to Menden the first time to pay for the first used Caterpillar machine. The second was bought in Finland and the third in Italy.

Lo! The business was registered from the start, but it excluded me. All things were bought in his name. How blind I was! All these things happened, even the plot of land we bought together ended up in his name. In the end, all the things I thought were important suddenly ceased to be important, and I lost everything. I had to pay back the loans from the banks but did not benefit from anything.

They painted me as being so black, such a bad person, you can't imagine. I became very depressed and lost so much weight. They talked me into believing that I was a bad person.

One day, Vivian came to visit us at Grevenbroich where I was staying. She wept and was so sad at seeing me in that condition. At some stage, I was psychologically believing that I really was bad and that was the beginning of my psychological breakdown.

By this time, I was beginning to know that all was not well. There was no hand-hold, no pillar to support me, and this maternal challenge had its hold on me. It was as if fate had singled me out.

In many respects, I felt unimportant, unaccepted and rejected. Funnily, I became absorbed into an increasingly unbearable situation. The maternal delay added to my fight, my misery and my loss of belief in me. Chika was to be adopted by us, but at a late stage my ex relationship withdrew his support, due to his family pressure and because we had so many other commitments.

I felt much better after the separation from my ex-relationship, and Chika stayed with my older sister Da Angela.

However, some time later when I was ready to go and officially adopt her and bring her to Germany, she was struck down with a high fever. Sadly, after doing all they could to save her, she died, due to the poor medical facilities at home.

We decided that only a few of us should know about this because of my mom. My mom had become so attached, and we knew it would have broken her heart. For this reason, only a very few people in the compound knew, so that no-one would accidentally break the news to my mom. We just told her that Chika was with us. May her soul and the souls of the departed rest in peace, Amen.

This news broke me down. Fortunately, Hagen, my new and wonderful husband (see later), saw my pain, and immediately made arrangements for us to visit a priest. We arranged this through an internet contact; we finally gained an appointment with Rev. Dr. Nwoko in Bremen through the late Sr. Judith. This meeting helped me a lot. I am a psychologist but could not heal myself. Gradually I got deeper into my prayers and my environment was healthy. I thank God for my Hagen and parents, for my family Adannem, Daa Ange, Vivian, Chinwe Obasi and the Rev. Sr. Gloria, and others.

Who are these people I call mine?

What have I done to earn these?

I could go on and on to ask questions, to which I know some answers and most I buried and pretended it was not happening to me.

I swallowed a lot, and got scorned, ridiculed and caricatured.

I suffered depression, but I fought it with the help of prayers, writing, reading and good family and friends.

Today, when I look back, I call them wasteful years, unproductive and just waste, waste and waste. And praying then became a problem, because I blamed God for allowing all these things to happen to me.

Why did I not opt out earlier? I did not know why until on that fateful day, when everything came to an end.

Sad Feelings

"A little more persistence, a little more effort, and what seemed hopeless failure may turn to glorious success"

- Elbert Hubbard.

Was I to cry, to scream.

Well in situations like this, shit happens,

When he came to pick me up at the airport, I thought all was ok,

He told me that he was leaving me.

What flashed through my mind was, Uuuu!

What will people think of me?

It was only people and their gossip I thought of,

These same thoughts, that made me forget 'Me',

I was in pain,

I remembered this woman in me, with lots and lots of stumbling blocks.

I let myself be defined by people's opinions,

I lost my Identity, and did not realise who I was,

Imagine this woman, who fought the agony of immigration, the bliss of maternity, now reduced to nothing, to a ghost. I had my papers, I was not looking for anything other than to be happy. I met what I did not bargain for.

2014 - according to German 'war es soweit', it was time,

He packed up and went.

Anyone in my situation, could feel what I felt,

confusion, a roller coaster and all that accompanies bad feelings.

I thought of all that had happened yet could not come to any conclusion. I was not at this moment thinking about God, what I thought of God was 'Why me?'. I did not seek answers. I had entered a hole again and depression set in. I got myself locked out, isolated and was thinking of ending it all.

I was then working at Barbara Haus, Caritas Haus in Grevenbroich. I did not have any other option other than to ask for one week's leave. This I was granted. In this one week many transformations happened. I spoke to Da Franca, Vivian. I then spent two days with Sister Gloria, who counselled me. I got back to work and decided to resign. I started thinking of relocating, because I needed to regain myself, refresh and start over again.

In this one week, I found myself spiritually longing for God. I started fasting and praying and gradually, gradually revived.

In Search of a 'Good Enough' Environment

Over the years I had worked in several work environments and places - hospitals, homes, care homes etc. At sometimes during my working life, I have suffered from a lack of acceptance, either because other people thought that I had a 'foreign' accent or that I was not speaking proper German. Although people do not often talk about institutional racism, a lot of foreigners still go through this on a daily basis.

But what should I do in such difficult times? I believed that searching until I obtained something good was a better way.

I obtained a new job at the Intensive Pflege Hamacher in Cologne, then moved after five months to the Laticia Intensive Pflege, just outside of Cologne. I resigned from this position when I met my present husband, Hagen, and got a job with Haus am Barkhof in Osterholz Scharmbeck. There I met some amazing people at Group IV, who were working with semi-coma and coma patients. I loved it. I had changed my workplace so many times in search of such a close-to-perfect job.

The change I want to see is an environment where everyone, regardless of gender and background, feels welcome and safe, where sexual harassment or discrimination will not impede great talent from producing great impact

Eventually, I find myself today working with Karin Burwitz, a woman with a good heart, who understands me, does not allow or encourage any kind of discrimination, and provides good nursing treatment to everyone. I work with her full-time, have a family and do my private study, all with ease. Thank you, Karin, the best employer anyone would love to have. I love working, because she creates an atmosphere that makes it impossible for anyone to say 'no' when she needs me to help.

The Gossip

"Most of the important things in the world have been accomplished by people who have kept on trying when there seemed to be no hope at all"

- Dale Carnegie.

I suffered a lot,
The remotest suffering ever,
The stigma, that was 'My Savage'
Mouths got loose on me,
Names and talks,
were heavily levied against me,
I sank into oblivion,
I regretted 'being me',
And lost 'me'.

Who are mine
This question came back,
hunting me again, crowded in my thoughts,
Made me miserable.
Days I did not see the outside,
was in constant touch with Da Franca, sister Gloria and Vivian,

They watered me, pampered me with preaching
of the stories of God,
Stories of those who have made it today.

I believed God forgot me,
Or rather, that God was punishing me,
I could not understand.

Is this a curse or what?

I learn from the teachings of Don Miguel Ruiz,
which says that don't take anything personally.
Nothing others do is because of you. What others
say and do is a projection of their own reality, their
own dream. When you are immune to the opinions and actions of others, you won't be the victim
of needless suffering.

PART 4

SIX IVF ATTEMPTS AND JOURNEYS

"We must accept finite disappointment,
but never lose infinite hope"

- Martin Luther King, Jr.

In the chapter I wrote in *The Perfect Migrant*, I spoke my heart out regarding a bitter journey which many married couple are confronted with today. I went down this lane and I know the pain that goes with it.

'What did I do wrong in life?', that was my question. This previous relationship that I had, I hate talking about it, because it had only pain.

We had been together for six months and nothing had happened. I became worried and had to seek out a gynaecologist who, after both normal and extra checks, told me there was no problem. I was ready at that time to go through any procedure, I had had two fibroid operations which were to the doctor very insignificant, but I needed to rule out every situation.

I went to my gynaecologist for a third time. She refused to attend to me and asked me to bring my partner in, saying there was nothing wrong with me. He initially hesitated and I had to inform the doctor that he was refusing. She told me flatly that she was not going to see me anymore, nor refer us for further help, unless she saw him and arranged for further tests to be conducted.

At that threat he decided reluctantly to follow me back in. The gynaecologist explained everything to him and gave us a referral to go to the university teaching hospital in Düsseldorf. The fertility test was undertaken with him and once the results were through that was when it dawned on him what the problem was. He cried, and I told him that we are both in this together.

There now followed a series of unsuccessful treatments for him, before we were able to go onto our first IVF trial, because that was now the only option left for us.

IVF (in-vitro fertilisation) is a kind of assisted reproductive technology. It is perhaps an artificial way to get pregnant. It is a process that involves removing a woman's egg (ova) after hormone-induced treatment, on the 14th day of the cycle. This may involve removing one or more ova under sedation, and they are then fertilised and cultured for 1-3 days or more depending on the ethics of the country involved (Medical dictionary). The fertilised egg is then replanted in the woman.

This was not easy for us. We did not have any success, so after two or three attempts in Düsseldorf we went to Cologne, Essen and then to Spain, but all to no avail. The same procedure and the same painful feeling afterwards. The pains and psychological torture, the financial cost and everything associated with it. I went through all of these. I was just saving up and was ready to go anywhere. During one of the attempts, a doctor told us that sometimes the egg may be perfect, and the sperm can fertilise it, but in its weak state the danger is it not holding and aborting.

I died many times in thought and came back, as I was not only going through this pain, I also had fingers pointed at me from his sister. She was very impatient. She had a habit of putting heads together and insinuating situations. She could fabricate things and make them look so real. I did not know which pain was worse. The failure of the IVF or what his sister tried to make out of my life. She terrorised my life, hunted me and made sure we fell apart. She said that I was too old and couldn't give her brother a child. Funny, how we humans point fingers at others. She knew her brother had issues, but...

I was completely lost, lost and never wanted to be found again. Yes, not only lost, but we separated and that was it again.

UNEXPECTED OUTCOME

It was actually in 2008 that the real journey began. Little did I know where these journeys were leading me to and the pains that were to accompany them. Yes, I went through this painful journey with this ex-guy six times. I found myself believing that I was cursed. They even called me a witch! I lost faith, I lost hope, and I became depressed, but I learnt to seek the face of God and that was actually my healing.

My actual healing, though hard then to judge, started when these wasteful eight years of nightmares was over, when that terrible man left my life.

I had been writing about it, documenting it all, and that was a good therapy for me.

Bernard Williams once said that there was never a night or a problem that could defeat sunrise or hope. I found a lot of comfort in this message.

CONFLICT SETS, THE LOST ME, WHO AM I?

"I can be changed by what happens to me,
But I refused to be reduced by it".

"You may not control all the events that happen to you, but you can decide not to be reduced by them"

- Maya Angelou.

This question haunted me. I could not even
Identify with my name. When called, I saw two
different people, a woman and a name,

Two things that had nothing in common but
were intertwined.

in a broken relationship, broken stories, empty
and void life...

Who am I?

I looked into the mirror to look for answers,

Answers I will never find,

Doubts of this kind stole my mind,

In seeking who I really am.

I sit alone most times,

encapsulated and consumed,

In worries of who am I.

Loneliness of mind,

A trait to sanity,

A thorn bird, perching with no nest,

A stealer of peace.

Stole my peace,

Anger beyond compare

Funny Images crowd my thoughts.

Who am I?

Lingered.

Lost in doubts.

Quest for IVF,

Failures, woes

These were my stories, nothing good to tell except woes.......

oh my God, I was about to quit, but I could not....

The Holy Bible became my companion through some of the darkest moments of my life.

PART 5

MEETING HAGEN CHANGED MY LIFE.

September 2012, very memorable.

One door closing in March 2012 and then another door opening in September, glory to God.

Our Supermarket Shopping

He came when I thought all was lost
My lost confidence,
Me was gone,
Thought I lost me.
But he came
and my life changed.
He found me.

When I most probably had made up my mind to settle into the single life and single status, to make my career and have a child, little did I know what God had in plan for me. In my place, Mbaise, where I come from, marriage and motherhood seem customary, a massive difference to the plans I had then.

I met this man, my husband Hagen, and that was God's way.

How did I meet my partner? I would like to describe my partner and present-day husband as if I was in a fairy tale.

I wanted to go shopping. I arrived and got myself a shopping trolley. Inside the shop, I started to do my shopping, step by step. When suddenly another shopping trolley ran into mine. The gentleman apologised for his carelessness and so we went our separate shopping ways.

When I was finished, at the point of paying, I saw him again, but did not recognise his presence. When I had paid and was going towards the exit, I saw someone in front of me, standing close to the door.

I continued outside to where I had parked my car and started loading my purchases into the boot. Suddenly I noticed a huge tall man, a German, standing beside me. He tried to make some jokes, to remind me that he was the guy who had run into my shopping trolley.

"Oh", I said, but still I did not understand what he wanted from me. "Yes?", I asked in a kind of tuneful "yeah?" I asked him, "How may I help you?". He started smiling. His smile was very warm and cordial. He kind of attempted to start a conversation with me.

Honestly speaking, I was not forthcoming then. I prayed secretly that he would leave me alone. But he continued in every way to initiate a conversation. He talked to me like someone he had met before.

Before I knew it we were conversing. He told me of his broken life, things that were meant for someone you have known a long while. He said a lot to me and I had pity for him.

Continuously we had synchronised our purchases in the shop, step-by-step in our individual trolleys until we reached the cashier but did not notice what we actually had in our trolleys. Our conversation was like a dream. We did not notice that time had passed by. At the cashier, everyone paid for their purchases and together we went into the car park to our cars to load our purchases. When returning the shopping trolleys, our conversation continued.

It was strange, I had the feeling that we had known each other for ages. I think we talked for over an hour. We now had our telephone numbers exchanged and he arranged to call me. When I got home with my purchases, I could not wait for the telephone to ring. It did not take him long to call, but I felt it was forever. We talked on the phone about when our trolleys collided. Our conversation went into the second round. In conversation, he told me how it came to the trolley crash. He had seen me in the car park when he was shopping, and it hit him like a bomb. Only he did not know how he should address me. Because my appearance had indeed struck him, yet at the same time he was unsettled because he was not sure how I was going to react to him. Thus came the idea of a trolley crash during shopping.

I am so happy and thank God for the fact that my life has about-turned so abruptly. He had also taken his purchases home and realised that he had not bought what he needed and what he had bought he didn't need. The feeling hit us both like lightning. From then on, we talked for hours every day. Even our relatives could not reach us anymore and they had already started to worry as our phone lines were constantly busy. So, our fairy tale started.

MY LIFE CHANGED

"Love recognizes no barriers, it jumps hurdles, leaps fence, penetrates walls to arrive at its destination full of hope (Maya Angelou).

Hagen my husband, my hope,
With you my life is complete,
God restored me through you.

In the days of my darkest hours,
Surrounded every day with negative thoughts,
And people.
I languished and was amassed with dark thoughts.

I lost me, and never thought I was going to find
me again!
These days of my pit hole lives,
Deep in a pit I cried to God,
I sought for love, peace and a home.
He heard me,
I suddenly saw a hand thrusting through the pit,
Wanting to pull me out,
This voice was very passionate,
very subtle, in his words,
All I heard was someone whispering and saying,
'Let me be your voice, let me be your pillow,
let me shoulder you,
Further he said,'
Come with me,
Take my hand,
I will lead you out, for your dark days are over,
Your sun has set,
trees are forming new figs,
flowers are flowering,
and gone are your pains.

Come my love he did not stop,
I will love you,
come with me to a place
we will build our world on God,
sing our love songs,

And tell our own stories.
Come where we can be together,
Wrap our hands, smile and kiss,
Come.

Our relationship developed

The development of our relationship was just as dreamlike as getting to know each other. A few months later I flew, as planned, for Christmas to my family in Nigeria for four weeks. Everyone in my family was so curious, everyone wanted to know everything and see pictures of him. My mom and the whole family immediately took him to their hearts and we were again busy talking on the phone. Actually, it was a nice four weeks for Christmas in the home, but also the longest time because my impatience and longing became stronger and stronger to see him again.

While at home with my family, he spoke and planned with my older sister Angela to get the measurement of my finger for an engagement ring. They planned this together and my sister remained true to her promise to him and did not disclose anything to me.

It was planned to be a surprise on my arrival back in Germany.

And the surprise paid off.

THE PROPOSAL AT DÜSSELDORF AIRPORT

When I returned to Germany in January 2013, he proposed marriage to me at the airport in Düsseldorf. Everyone knew about it, but not me. Even my family in Nigeria was privy to what my husband-to-be was up to. Also, everyone at the airport was in the picture. Even the wedding was like a fairy tale because my husband picked me up royally with a white carriage. To this day, people are still talking about our wedding, whether from the church or from the locality and our guests as well. My greatest wishes have all been fulfilled unsurpassed. We are like a unit. There is no white or black, no left or right. There is only us as one. You could say a fairy tale newly written for us.

"Only one thing was left, my most intimate thoughts".

True love at play

> *"We make the world we live in and shape our own environment"*
>
> *- Orison Swett Marden.*

Suddenly, I started finding a sense and meaning in life. I laughed and felt happy again. All this happened so quickly. We grew every day in love, we spent most of our time together when we were not working. Despite the initial fears I had about going into another relationship, everything seemed perfect. God is so good.

This guy was determined to share his life with me.

First Visit to His Parents

"Forget yourself. Become one with eternity. Become part of your environment"

- Yayoi Kusama.

I was so scared, being a black person and not knowing what was going to be their reaction towards me. I bought an orchid flower, for that was customary. It was in January 2013 when I came back from my trip to Nigeria that we both came on this visit to his parents.

He drove and while I was sitting there, my heart pounded. I just did not know, I wanted it to be quick and over. The journey lasted three good hours, and during that time he tried to calm me down, to let me know that his parents looked forward to meeting me.

The meeting went well, I brought as tradition demanded a flower for his mother. And my first impression was great and that is God's way.

At this stage I confided in my sister Da Franca, Chioma and the Rev. Sister Gloria.

I relocated to Bremen in 2014, it was an easy move for me. I did not find the thought of going there difficult. After he talked to me about some family stuff, I knew immediately that his parents would be needing us.

In fact, I did not hesitate to move with him down to Bremen.

"The ideal of behaviourism is to eliminate coercion: to apply controls by changing the environment in such a way as to reinforce the kind of behaviours that will benefits everyone"

- B.F. Skinner.

I accepted his family wholeheartedly and it was love at first sight. Because of my humble background, things that happened in his family were very challenging. But I saw it not as a challenge, but as a test of my faith and what God can do through us if we truly surrender and believe in Him.

We went through a tough time, due to some family chaos that led to his parents losing their two companies, and nearly losing the family house as well. The situation led to my father-in-law filing for bankruptcy. This was another trial in my life. I had asked God to send me to where I was needed. I guess, I am where I am needed the most.

My husband fought a noble son's fight to redeem the face of his family. Thank God we were able to help them, to an extent, to get through those tough times.

The hollow is still there and to God be the glory.

MAKING BREMEN MY HOME

Bremen, Germany is my home. My story is never complete without expressing my thanks to Germany and my now second home Lilienthal Niedersachsen, Bremen. Bremen is a Hanseatic city in North-Western Germany. Lilienthal is for me Bremen, but people laugh when I say that.

This home has given me comfort and made me smile again. It was not easy initially, but in the end we all had reasons to smile again. Glory to God. Stay true to where you find yourself. Make it a home and be a good reason and not a hindrance.

I have reason to smile again

Our court wedding, April 2014

*"I believe in an India of pluralism and diversity,
not of religious bigotry and caste politics. I believe
in an India that is secure in itself and confident
of its place in the world, an India that is a proud
example of tolerance, freedom and hope for the
downtrodden"*

- Shashi Tharoor.

I am a person of the lost time,
I had one of the lucks,
I lost me,
But he found me,
Turned me round,
And we were married.

Und Nun, bin ich zufrieden (Now am happy).

We had this at a small family court with my then colleagues from Haus am Barkhof Osterholz Scharmbeck, in Germany. They gave me a grandiose surprise that I never expected. Hartmund and his wife, our neighbours, were our patrons. My mother in-law prepared for the reception, which was at home with the family.

My sister was always present, and I thought that was the best. But that was yet to come.

When God is at Work

Our church wedding, August 2014

We were on holiday in Cyprus, but little did I know that my husband had planned to buy another additional wedding ring for the church wedding. He is now a converted Catholic, formerly Anglican. All went to the glory of God.

On one of our outings from the hotel where we stayed, he had already gone the previous day alone to the town, made all the arrangements and just led me there. What I saw was "Wow"!

I chose this wedding ring of 585 gold, that matched his very beautiful ring, and there and then our names were engraved upon them. At the same time, we chose a date for our church wedding, while praying that it would not clash with the church's programme in Lilienthal.

Our church wedding was on the 30th of August 2014. The ceremony began at 12.00 noon German time. We had the Christian Gospel Choir from Bremen who sang for us. They sang the church to euphoria, singing the most amazing songs like Aka Jehovah (God's Hand), O Happy Day, and others.

Me with my parents-in-law

My mother in-law organised for the hairdresser and paid for it. Since we're-located here, I have never had a dull moment. I found myself adjusting so easily to everyone, the environment and my parents-in-law.

My wedding gown was chosen by my mother-in-law and I, as German tradition forbids men from seeing the wedding gown before the actual wedding. I loved my wedding dress, it had a band at the back and was sleeveless. We chose a long veil and other accessories that went with it. My favourite colours are white and pink, and everything matched perfectly.

My wedding bouquet was chosen by my husband, in pink and white, my favourite colours.

The bridesmaids and pageboy were perfectly well-dressed. All were from the family. My sister Vivian and her husband Branko were our best man and best lady of the day and at the same time our patrons.

Leading up to that day, I could not sleep properly for joy. I imagined a lot and truly the Lord is mighty indeed.

At exactly 11.30 am my father-in-law drove me to the church and guided me into the church where he handed me over to my husband, who was already waiting in the church, in Hirte Katholische

Kirche, Lilienthal. It drizzled a bit, but I saw it as a blessing. It only lasted a few minutes and everywhere was soon dry again.

Our then Priest, Rev. Fr. Lange, delivered a perfect sermon that was very touching.

"Wenn zwei Menschen sich ineinander verliebt, gibt keine Unterschied mehr" (when two people are in love, there seems to be no difference in colour, and others, the only thing that matters is character and the good heart of the couple, they are like salt and pepper).

We exchanged vows and it was one moment that I will never forget.

Many of our family members, friends and well-wishers attended the wedding and all were delighted and still speak about the beauty of the wedding even to today. DaFranca, Da Caro all from London.

The Wonders of God

The wedding ceremony

After the wedding, we waited outside, and I looked out for a car that would carry us to the reception hall. We had booked a hall at Meyerdierks Garten, a very beautiful location also in Lilienthal, about 10 kilometres away from our church and very accessible for visitors.

Suddenly, I saw a white horse and carriage coming along the road and truly speaking I never associated it with our wedding. I probably thought it was some kind of local celebration going on. The carriage stopped directly opposite us and my husband kissed me and simultaneously everyone started to clap and dance, my family and friends were all clapping, and all congratulated me. It was all as if in a movie.

I asked if someone could tell me what was going on here. The fact was that everyone knew about the plan except me. Wow! I was so happy. I never could never have imagined that, but my husband made me feel more like a queen. I give God all the glory.

This is Hagen and Me

The minute it dawned on me that we were about to go to the wedding reception driven in a horse and carriage, tears of joy filled my eyes. The mass service had gone on longer than planned, and that was to tell you how marvellous our God is. The priest was so happy, and my uncle Rev. Fr. Hyacient Ibeh had also come from Belgium to join in officiating the mass.

At exactly 2pm the horse and carriage started its long procession to the reception hall, with us proudly being carried along

MY WEDDING - A DAY TO REMEMBER

The horse and carriage drove us along the street, with photographers running behind us, cars and entourage all behind us, and we had a guard in front of us. Before we got to the hall, most of our guest were already waiting with a glass of wine in hand, all lined up in a roll of honour to usher us into the hall.

You never could imagine how I felt. Me, after being so lost. I said a silent prayer, praised and thanked God.

We had about 150 guests, a mixture of both Africans and Germans. Our priest honoured our invitation, which normally they don't do, and we were so happy that he did.

We had lovely food which was well cooked and beautifully served, and everyone had plenty to drink and eat. There was a mixture of African and German music playing, with everyone dancing, being happy and merry.

My niece and nephew composed a song and sang it for us. It was all so emotional that most of us cried. What a day!

A Poem to My Husband

The day we met at the supermarket,
I knew you were God sent,

I felt lucky and blessed,
I am blessed indeed.
When I got home,
I let out tears that ran down my cheek,
Grief that needed to be let out.
The poured down,
And I refused to wipe them.
God exists,
How lucky I am,
To see these beautiful things,
Happen in my lifetime.
All because you came into my life.
I love you ever and ever.
Ich werde dich immer und immer wieder heiraten (would marry you again and again).

Mein Herz jubelt (My heart rejoices).
    das du mein Leben so bereichert hast (You have enriched my world)
    das machte es leichter für mich (and that makes it so easy for me).

    I will forever love you.
    Thank you, God.

Our wedding cake was a fruit cake, beautifully designed and especially made for us.

When it was time to cut the cake, our MC, Mr Kenneth Eze, announced it all. He was a very wonderful speaker, Author and entertainer, wow, there was never a dull moment. A few of my colleagues from work came. In short, what a day. It was a lavish reception. Some songs moved me to tears. "It's a beautiful day" from U2, Stone Roses, Helene Fischer, Bryan Adams and many others.

> *"Everyone has her own love life. Everyone*
> *has a dream to get a perfect life partner.*
> *But this is not so easy in real life. In fact,*
> *one doesn't love. It happens"*
>
> *- Katrina Kaif*

Happiness Unmeasured

OUR BUNDLE OF JOY, 2016
He was my huge hope,
God sent,
A counsellor, my comforter.
He loved me, admired even my shortcomings,
He treated me like a real woman.
And gave me my lost confidence.

He made me bold with his love,
And cleaned my tears.

Wann ich traurig bin, hältst du mich fest,
was in mein Leben noch nicht passiert war

(When am sad you held me tight, what has never happened to me before).

I melt in your arm and start to live again. I was so amazed at his character, the way he assimilated himself into our culture. He saw my people as his people, ate all our foods, enjoyed everything about us. A very genuine person. His parents accepted me fully, and I loved them so much in return. My family love him too.

What human can truly know God's plans? God understood my case, and guided me to this way.

Taking Time to Thank God

My life still has ups and downs, but I take it one day at a time and I just hope that I can be the best that I can possibly be, not only for myself, but also young people that are out there today that need someone to look up to

I said to God as I looked up,
I was ruined, desolate and lost,
His love found me.
I was tormented, jarred at, judged,
He never judged me.

I bring thanks to you Lord,
My faithful God,
My love is for You.
My God you picked me from my lowest pit,

Cleaned me and fixed my broken self,
You are the most precious in the Universe,
Holiest of all.

Not minding my wretched and imperfect person,
From imperfect place,
You still sent me Hagen,
My heart is full of praise.
THANK YOU, GOD.
FOREVER I AM GRATEFUL.

A Perfect Team

They are white skinned,
I am dark skinned,
All these never mattered,
As we took no notice of them.

They loved me,
I loved them,
We shared,
We hoped,
We fought together,
When we lost we lost together?
And when we win we won together.
We spoke the same voice.

We respect one another,
We leaped,

We climbed,
We fall,
We cry and smile together.

We are
The perfect team.

WHEN OUR DESIRE TURNS HARD

How did my desire for children develop? My heartfelt desire for children became louder and louder. Unfortunately, I was not allowed to achieve this from a medical point of view naturally without the help of IVF, a medical wonder. I have always wanted to be a good mother. To give what I have. I have tried natural ways and many treatments for my desire to have children. In all this time, my husband supported me and stood behind me. We are both very happy, for our goal all together and for each other has come true.

When the Journey Becomes Tough

PEOPLE WHISPER BEHIND
They did not know my journey,
But they talked me down,
They have not walked my path,
Yet they were blasting me,
They have not asked why?
They have passed verdict,

They never weighed me,
They Pulled me down.
They judged me,
They hung me,
They never could imagine my miles,
They never knew how far I had gone,
My journeys,
My struggles,
My falls, my woes and my untold stories,
But they wrote me off.
Off, off and blotted me out.

LESSONS FOR YOU READER

My advice is to never succumb to the challenges of life, seek and you will find, follow your mind, do that which makes you happy. It may take years, but at least it will be nice that you did not die with your dreams unfulfilled. But don't allow anyone to define you, based on your past. You are the only one who can stop 'you' from climbing further, so don't stop on your way to success.

The first step towards success is taken when you refuse to be a captive of the environment in which you first find yourself.

I would like to thank all who have supported me in my life journeys. Thank you, my audience and readers of this book. We all are in a journey, our paths to our success will always remain different.

Whatever, follow your dreams, don't forget your roots, where you come from, embrace, support, integrate and learn something from your new environment. Anywhere could be home, it all depends on how we make our new environment.

Take a look at others who have gone through many challenges, know what you want, use your past failures as a guide towards your future. No failure should dictate your pace. People will talk, but no-one is perfect. I made many mistakes, had wrong relationships, failed many times, but held unto God, because I know my redeemer liveth.

Colour, race and tribe should not define where you marry or who you choose to live with. What matters is the person, the character, they rest with God, both of you can work it out. We must master and overcome our fears in order to overcome our captives. Speak out, let others share your downs, you may be helping someone.

The Importance of Networking

"You can't change the world; you can fix the whole environment. But you can recycle. You can turn the water off when you're brushing your teeth. You can do small things"

- Patti Smith.

My sister Vivian was very good at carrying everything along. She is a self-made talented artist, who started painting as a hobby. Today her paintings with a heavy African accent speak and tell of the tales and woes of Africa. She is a real example that we can still become what we are meant to be despite all challenges. She would invite me to most of her art exhibitions and she encouraged me to network. She said to me "I know you have a lot of books in you, perhaps....".

I was attending an event in Berlin in 2017. The event was run by African Women Europe, a network of women founded by a German based African woman called Joy Zenz. One of the speakers was Amina Chitembo the founder and owner of a UK based Publishing Company Diverse Cultures Publishing. Amina is a Book Writing Coach and Publisher. God used this professional to help me come out as an author.

As I write this book, I have co-authored three books, all with the help of Amina. I am also working on another book which will be released in 2019.

Not My Way

> *"A lot of people have their dreams and get knocked down and don't have things go their way. And you never give up hope,*

*and you really just hold on to it. Hard
work and perseverance. You just keep getting up
and getting up, and then you
get that breakthrough"*

- Robert Kraft.

"I vowed that nothing was going to stop me,
I vowed to make it,
To dare odds,
Learn from odds
To be wise,
And use my lessons of yesterday,
My falls and failures,
To love the beauty of God
And cling stronger to God.
For with Him,
My confidence came back,
I learnt the tools to,
Ignore, be focused
Fight and never run away.
From challenges,
From people and their tongues.

For Tongues were mere nothing,
A mere way of pulling words,
Confusing,
to suit their audience.
And bring you down.

Say no to them,
All you have is YOU!
You are Unstoppable.

> *Thank God, all was not lost,*
> *I found me at last,*
>
> *"Made the most of myself…*
> *For that is all there is of me."*
>
> *- Ralph Waldo Emerson.*

SUBSCRIBE TO MY BLOG:

Get more training, tools and tips from me and other:

https://www.claram.com

I will see you there.

- Clara

Acknowledgment

I have so many people to thank for supporting and encouraging me all through my life journey. To Almighty God and my family, whose support has been immeasurable. Thank you, Mama, Papa, Dedé, Da França, Da Ange, Cos, Pau Pau and family, Ugochi, you all are great.

Thank you Bolaji Aina, you are just amazing for helping me all through my time in Germany and thank you to Dr. Wolfgang whose help saw me through to Germany. Also, thank you Bunmi Korikor and family (Falusi) (School of Nursing, Akure).

Thank you to the Agunnia family (my second family), and to my childhood sister Dr. Vivian Timothy whose motto is 'It is never too late to live your dream'. Vivian Chioma, as we call her, is a motivator, a pusher. Vivian, you personally mean a lot to me.

I thank God for my loving husband Hagen Meierdierks, whose love and encouragement has meant so much to me. Hagen, your rewards are uncountable, you are just a blessing designed from God for me.

My parents-in-law Christa and Alfred Meier-dierks and my precious child, my bundle of joy Shanaya Ezinne Chinagorom Meierdierks, who from day one has played and supported me in her adoring ways.

Thank you sister Gloria my mentor, Sister Bernett, Mr. Hon. Obasi and family, Bro Chibuike and family, Mr. Vitus Obasi and family, Rev. Fr. Hyacinth Ibe and others.

My cousins, nieces, nephews and uncles De Vin and De Nich Uwazie, my late uncle Mr. Nich Nwachukwu, and De Bernard, De Francis, De Charly, the Rev. Dr. Inno and others, my aunties, in-laws and well-wishers.

Da Caro Osuagwu, Auntie Mary Jane Ememe and family, Da Theresa Nwogu and family, Auntie Rose Franchesca Uche and family, my beloved Ulunne Angee Ndukwu and family, my brothers, Chimeka, Ugochi and family, Nneka, Chinyere, Miracle, Amarachi and to many more whose names are not mentioned here.

Thank you to my parents, the Late Mr and Mrs Patrick Uwazie; Mama and Papa thank you for bringing me here.

Thank you to Mr John and Mrs Helen Spelman for giving your time to proof read through my work.

Thank you Goody Ogbuaja and family, Mr Remy Kaduru and family, Auntie Rose and family, Familia Christopher Chukwu, and others for encouraging me. Thank you to my cousin Chris Chima and family.

Thank you, Germany, and thank you to my Lilienthal, my second home, for providing the environment to live my dream.

Thank you Rev. Father Lange (Lilienthal), Gemeinde Lilienthal / Katholische Kirche Gute Hirt and OHZ.

Thank you Ijeoma Habicht, Yesni Wiryena, Wetterstein Altenheim, Augsburg, Lukas KH in Neuss, Etienne KH, Barbara Haus Caritas Grevenbroich, Mr. Häke, Fr. Marlies Keller, Haus am Barkhof, Advertus Intensiv Pflege, Karin Burwitz IHP Intensive Pflege. Thank you, Herr Jurgen, (Valerius Academy, Duisburg) and thank you everyone.

Because of you all (and those whose names are not mentioned here), I was able to come this far.

Although I have been writing my life story, I owe my courage to come out to speak and overcome my fears first at an 'Afrikanische Woche Augsburg' (African Week) through the help of my sister Vivian.

Thank you Women Empowerment (Sarah Sonni) Munich and all other women in the group. Thank you, Positive Life Global Empowerment E.V. Hamburg, (Mrs Ngozi Utoh-Samuel). Thank you AWE (Joy), thank you CWO Bremen and NCWO, thank you Rev. Fr. Ihuoma and Dr. Emeka. Thank you Rev. Sister Ebegbulem and Sr. Charity.

Thank you, Amina Chitembo, the publisher and someone who has now become my mentor and coach. She encouraged me to speak and write my story and helped me to I believe and trust in myself - and here I am today.

My Other Books

The Perfect Migrant – Co-author, May 2018

African Women in Europe – Contributor, 2018

Celebrating Diversity – Co-Author, October 2018

I am also in the process of writing my second solo book due out in 2019, it is entitled Yearning for a Child. Aimed at helping other parents who are struggling to have children.

Final Remarks

Firstly, thank you for taking time to read my book. Your reviews are important to me. So here is my request. If you enjoyed this book and learned something from it, you can help me in one or more of the following ways:

→ Go online, at www.amazon.co.uk or my website www.claram.com write a kind review.
→ Let us connect on LinkedIn: https://www.linkedin.com/in/clara-meierdierks-606001164/
→ Attend one of my trainings or seminars
→ Email me if I can be of any help with your training or awareness raising events at claram. author@gmail.com I do reply directly.
→ Get a copy of this book as a gift to your friend or family.
→ Continue to grow to the next level of your life and build the happy life and success you want.

THANK YOU.

About the Author

My name is Clara Meierdierks (née Uwazie). I was born in Nnarambia Ahiara, Mbaise, Nigeria, to the late Mrs Elizabeth Adanma Nneoha Uwazie and the late Mr. Patrick Uzodinma Uwazie. My mother gave birth to eight children in total.

I am qualified as a Nurse/Midwife, a Quality Manager (Cert.) and have a B.Sc.(Hons) in Health and Social Welfare and an M.Sc. in Psychology. I am also a Respiratory Care Practitioner, as well as being a speaker, a blogger and an author. I am in my late 40s and just so happy that I have recently discovered why I was born. Being an author has added so much more colour into my life. I am so happy.

At the moment I am working with semi-coma and coma patients utilising life support aids, and I must confess that working with such patients has helped to reshape my life in a very positive way. These experiences have brought me closer to the realities of life.

I am very active in the field of women's organisations and empowerment. I am a founder member of CWO Bremen, and a member of the CWO at a national level. I am also an active member of 'African Week', an event which is held every year in Augsburg and where I have had the opportunity to speak on the causes of people having to take flight and immigration causes, and their likely solutions. My thanks go to my sister Vivian, Margret Aulbach, Julia Kupa and lots of others who have helped me in these matters.

I love reading and writing. I also love seeing people happy, and I pray that those I may have offended should forgive me. I do not hold anything against anyone, because it is a burden to do so, and I love my peace.

I believe that we all are born to be creative and no matter where we find ourselves, or the challenges we go through in life, we should not leave God, for through prayers we get our strength and faith, and through faith and hard work, the sky will be our starting point.

Just like any other person, I have gone through many challenges and have fallen many times. I just believe in never quitting - fight, pray, pursue your dreams, and the universe will do the rest.

Praise for the Book

BY EVA KAMMLER

I met the author some years ago for the first time during an event in my catholic parish and it turned out that she had her roots in the eastern part of Nigeria. I was very happy meeting her because I had been working in the 70ies and the 80ies not in her home district, but in a neighbouring state in the east of Nigeria. I was familiar with Igbo traditions and culture. In fact, I value this part of my own history especially because I have learnt so much for my future life.

So, it is a pleasure and an honour for me to write a review of this book, which shows not only the story of an outer migration between two continents but talks about the long journey to one's self.

It shows that tradition can be both holding us warm when we feel chilled by events of our life and search for orientation and hold. And that tradition can be become a crucial burden when it prevents us from going the one- and only-way which God has thought to be our way. Which may be a narrow path separating us from the past and taking us to new horizons and a new understanding of ourselves.

This book shows how the author mastered the difficult times of her life. She looked for empowerment strategies and found them in prayers. The strong faith which is part of her Christian upbringing helped her finally to overcome the feeling of being abused and deceived by a partner who did not respect her on the basis of equality, who did not love her. She found her way out of such a destructive relationship. And she met finally a man who although not from her cultural background respects and loves her. She could find a family together with him and made herself a new home.

It is a moving story and at the same time a story which tells you not to forget the feeling for your own dignity which is God's gift to every single person.

May the reader learn from her story what it means to maintain self-respect and find the one and only path which was meant to be your path in life.

Cover Art

Dr. Vivian Timothy- Art Unleashed
Name: Self-Evolution
Acrylic on Canvas 60/80cm
Website: Art-Unleashed.Com
Description: Prose Self-Evolution

"Painting Myself Out of My Cage,
Liberating Myself From my fears and doubts,
Please! don't tell me I have arrived,
I am still on my journey to self,
Breaking free from the shackles of my past with my
Brush and colours.
Evolving as a person,
Still evolving,
Keep evolving."
- Dr. Vivian Timothy.